...My School...

My Friends

MB Macaw BOOKS

© Macaw Books

www.macawbooks.com

Printed in India

It was Jo's first day at her new school. She was feeling very nervous. 'I hope I can make friends here,' she thought.

There were both boys and girls in Jo's class. Some were plump and some were thin. Some were short and some were tall.

Jo's classmates greeted her warmly. 'Welcome to the class, Jo,' said a girl called Jean.

'It's is nice to meet you, Jo,' said Julie and Steve. Julie had short hair and Stevie had curls. Jo liked Julie and Stevie and Jean.

In class, Jo shared her seat with a girl named
Linda. Lisa and Rosie sat next to them.

Rosie was so funny! She was always made others laugh. Rosie and Jo had so much fun together!

In gym period, Jo made friends with a girl named Sue.
She could run faster than all the other boys and girls.

When Jo fell down and hurt her knee, a kind girl named Tessa comforted her. And that is how Jo and Tessa became friends.

In the art period, Jo made
friends with a boy named
Harry. Harry wore big glasses
and could draw very well.

Jo also became friends with Rita. Rita was very smart. She could solve any puzzle within minutes!

Jo also made friends with a boy named Todd. He had orange hair and made paper aeroplanes.

At recess, Jo and her friends flew Todd's paper planes. What great fun they had!

After school, Rosie and Jo walked
home together. They lived in the
same neighbourhood!

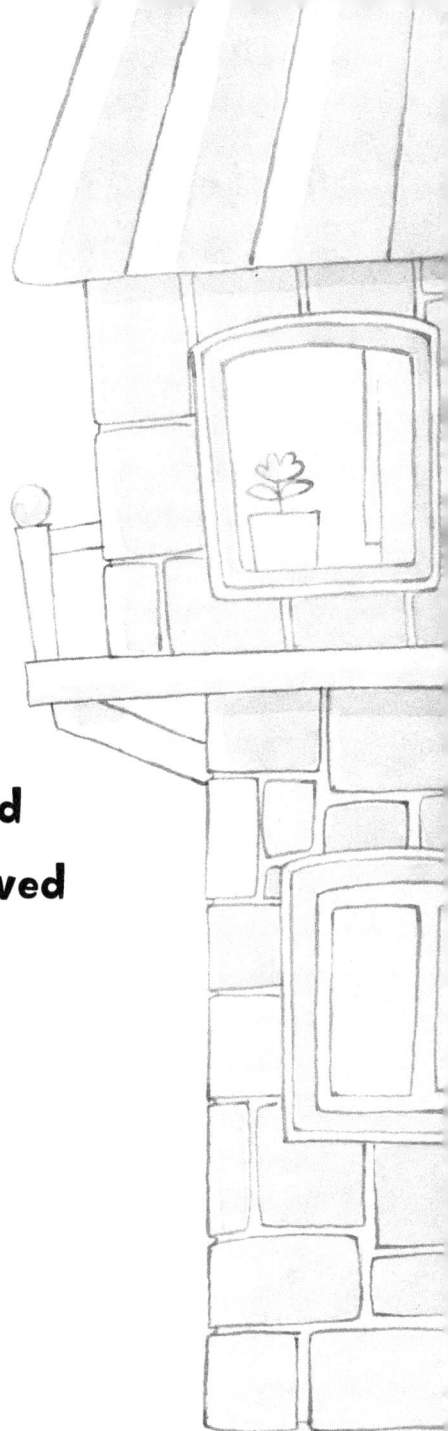

'See you tomorrow!' Rosie shouted from her bedroom window. Jo waved back at her happily.

At the end of the day, Jo felt very happy. She had made so many new friends. Jo could not wait to have more fun with them.

...My School...

My
Teacher

It was Teacher's Day. Miss Janet's students were very excited. They had planned a surprise for her.

When Miss Janet reached school in the morning, they waved at her. 'Good morning, Miss Janet!' they cried.

When Miss Janet entered the class, her students shouted, 'Happy Teacher's Day, Miss Janet!' Miss Janet was very surprised.

Tom and Sophie had brought a cake for her. Tessa gave her a doll and Liam had made her a nice drawing. 'Oh thank you, dear children!' said Miss Janet.

The students were on their best behaviour for Teacher's Day. They had learnt all the letters of the alphabet to make Miss Janet happy.

Soon the lesson began. 'Who can tell me a word that starts with A?' Miss Janet asked. 'Apple!' all the students cried together. 'Good job, kids!' said Miss Janet.

A apple

B bread

Next, it was time for their counting lesson. All the students had practiced their numbers for Teacher's day.

So when Miss Janet asked them to count from 1 to 10, no one forgot a number. Miss Janet clapped with joy!

In music class, Miss Janet taught them a new song. All the students sang along in tune. Not one child made a mistake.

The students had learnt a song for Miss Janet too. They sang it for her at the end of class. How happy she was!

During play time, the students and
Miss Janet played many games with
Miss Janet. She read a story to them.

Then they held hands and sang. Oh, how much fun they had together!

In the last period, Miss Janet said,
'You made me feel so special today!
And I have a gift for you too. I shall
take you to the zoo after school!'

The students had a great time with Miss Janet at the zoo. She showed them elephants and parrots and many other animals.

At the end of the day, Miss Janet was very glad. Her students truly loved her. And the students were glad too. They had the best teacher in the whole world!

www.ingramcontent.com/pod-product-compliance
Lightning Source LLC
LaVergne TN
LVHW082324080426
835508LV00042B/1531